FROM
DEATH
TO
LIFE

CHORAL SELECTIONS FOR HOLY WEEK AND BEYOND

Lillenas PUBLISHING COMPANY

KANSAS CITY, MO 64141

CONTENTS

It Is Finished

W. J. G. and GLORIA GAITHER

WILLIAM J. GAITHER
Arr. by Marty Parks

CD: 04

meet on____ Gol - goth - a's hill._____

The earth shakes with the force of the

con - flict;_____ The sun_____ re - fus - es to

bat-tle-fields of my own mak - ing,_____ I did-n't

know that the war had been won._____ Then I

heard that the King of all a - ges_____ had

Oo, King of all a - ges,_____

now, praise His name, I am free!

Now, praise His name, I am free! I am free!

Soloist join choir

And it is fin - ished! The bat - tle is

Lamb of God

T. P.

TWILA PARIS
Arr. by Tom Fettke

His Power Medley

Arr. by Joseph Linn

rest of my years.   I sought the Lord__ and He   gra-cious-ly an-swered.

He took a-way__ from me   my great-est fear.   He took a-way__ from me

my great-est   fear.

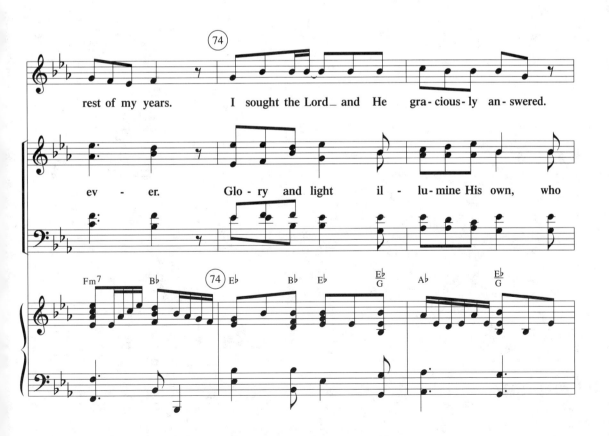

I Love You, Jesus

* A cappella preferred

S. R. A.

STEPHEN R. ADAMS
Arr. by Tom Fettke

I love You, Je - sus_____ for what You've done._____

I love You, Je - sus_____ for what You've done._____

cresc.

You've giv - en life to me,_____ set my spir - it free,

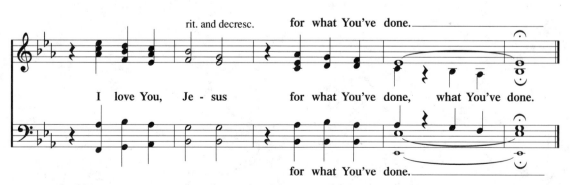

rit. and decresc. for what You've done._____

I love You, Je - sus for what You've done, what You've done.

for what You've done._____

Isaiah 53
<u>with</u> God Hath Provided a Lamb

Arr. by Tom Fettke

*"God Hath Provided a Lamb" (Linda Almond)

Narrator: In God's eyes He was like a tender green shoot, sprouting from a root in dry and sterile ground. But in our eyes there was no attractiveness at all, nothing to make us want Him. We despised Him and re-

jected Him—a man of sorrows, acquainted with bitterest grief. We turned our backs on Him and looked the other way when He went by. Yet it was our grief He bore; our sorrows weighed Him down. And we thought

His troubles were punishment from God for His own sins. We are the ones who strayed away like sheep!

34

We who left God's path to follow our own. Yet God laid on Him the guilt and sins of everyone of us (Isa. 53:2,3a,4,6, TLB).

*"Isaiah 53" (Linda Rebuck - Tom Fettke)

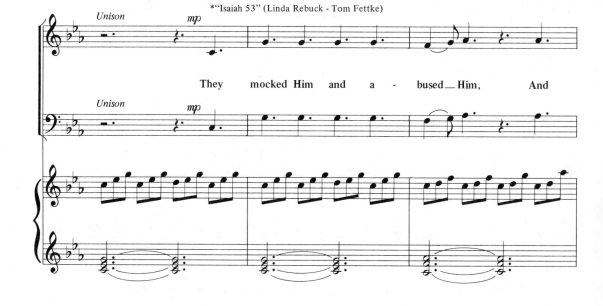

They mocked Him and a - bused—Him, And

looked the oth - er way. They scourged Him and ac -

cused___ Him; Yet noth-ing did He say. The

ones He loved con - demned Him; The Lamb made no re -

ply. He took our sins up - on ___ Him When they

led Him a-way to die.

Sing al-le-lu-ia! God hath pro-vid-ed a

Lamb. O sing al-le-lu-ia!

CD: 20

In tempo
♪. = ca. 56

rit.

"God Hath Provided a Lamb" (Linda Almond)
mf accented

God hath pro-vid-ed a Lamb.

Sar-ah was bar-ren, but

Basses (tenor opt.)

God prom-ised A-bra-ham: "Lo, I will give you a son._____

Your seed shall be as the sands of the sea; Through you I will bless ev-'ry

Lyrics:
one." Then God spake to Abraham: "Take thy son Isaac, Go

in-to the moun-tains a - bove. There on the al - tar of

CD: 21

sac - ri - fice lay him; Give Me the child of thy love."

Upon the mountains to the place of the sacrifice, Slowly they walked hand in hand _____ To lay on the altar the promise of Israel, Obeying God's __ command. _____ But there in the wilderness,

lo, a voice thun-dered; God spoke to His ser-vant a - gain:_____

CD: 23

(90) "Take not the life of thine on - ly son I - saac, For God hath pro - vid - ed a

(94) **Stronger** Lamb. _____ Sing al - le - lu - ia!

Unison

God hath pro - vid - ed a Lamb._____ O sing al - le -

lu - ia!_____ God hath pro - vid - ed a Lamb._____ O,

Lamb._____ Wea - ry and wan - der - ing down thro' the a - ges, Op -

CD: 24 2nd time

cued notes 1st time only

rit.

Freely

Accompaniment optional—a cappella preferred

pressed and af-flict-ed with - in;_____ No more the sac-ri-fice giv-en by man Could a-

tone for the e-vil of sin._____ God sent His on-ly Son Je-sus, Mes-

si-ah, To die on the al-tar of man._____ Once and for all the a-

CD: 25

(119) Slowly

tone-ment was made___ And God hath pro - vid - ed a Lamb.___

accel. poco a poco

cresc. a tempo ♩. = 56

(123) Very strong

Sing al - le - lu - ia! God hath pro-vid-ed a Lamb. ___ O

sing al - le - lu - ia! _____ God hath pro - vid - ed a

Lamb. He is the Lamb that God _____ pro -

vid - ed; He is the fi - nal sac - ri - fice. O, He is

wor - thy, praise — Je - ho - vah! Praise the Lord, hal-le - lu - jah! He is the

jah! Praise the Lord, hal-le - lu - jah! Praise the

Lord, hal - le - lu - jah! Hal-le-lu - jah!

O Calvary's Lamb

C. B., B. G. and T. G.
CHARLES BOSARGE, BILL GEORGE and TOMMY GREER
Arr. by Marty Parks

am,_____ I owe to Thee,_____ O_____

CD: 31   2nd time

CD: 29

Cal - v'ry's   Lamb.

Tenor solo **mp**   D.S.

And   when   mine

D.S.

Lamb. O Cal - v'ry's

Lamb, O Righ - teous One, for sin - ners died, whose sins were

28 Fuller

28 Choir: With deep emotion

Cal - v'ry's Lamb, Righ - teous One, Sin - ners died,

28

52

Resurrection Celebration
A Medley

**Including
It Is Finished
Resurrection
Because He Lives
Glorious Morning**

Arr. by Tom Fettke

*"It Is Finished" (Naish, Brown)

Light and bright ♩= ca. 69

Christ has won!_____ It was writ - ten of God's Son! For be - hold_____ the Lamb_____ has ful - filled God's

56

CD: 35

*"Because He Lives" (Gaither)

Lord is not here; He is a-live, He's not here! Christ is ris - en! God sent His

60

CD: 36 4th beat

*"Glorious Morning" (Dooley, McSpadden, Goss/Holck)

E - ter - ni - ty's war, fought through the a - ges, Comes to an end at Cal - va - ry's cross; And the

lives.

no stone could seal. Oh, glo - ri - ous morn - ing, the world has a Sav - ior; He is a - live and His truth is re - vealed. Oh,

CD: 37

Risen for Me

W. G. OVENS and
GLADYS W. ROBERTS

TOM FETTKE

68

My Faith Still Holds

W. J. G. and GLORIA GAITHER

WILLIAM J. GAITHER
Arr. by Mosie Lister

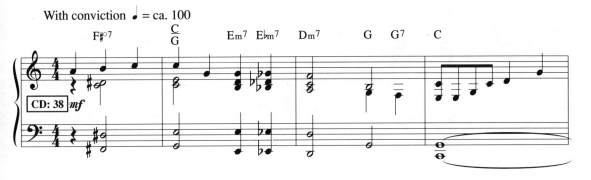

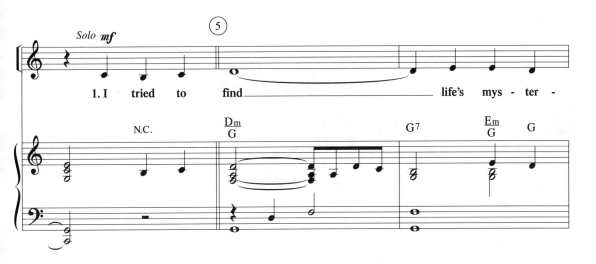

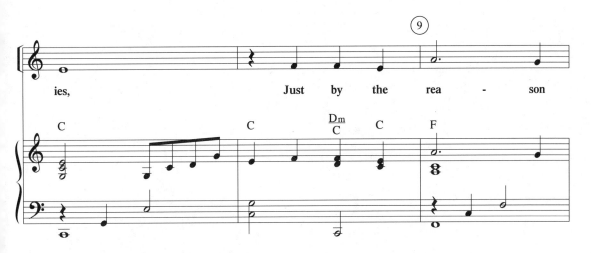

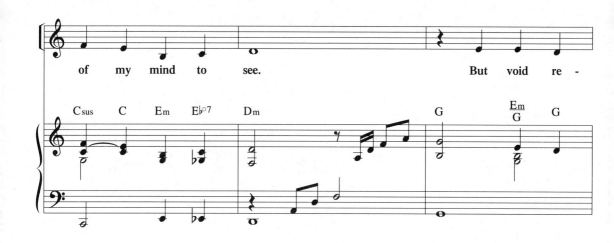

of my mind to see. But void re -

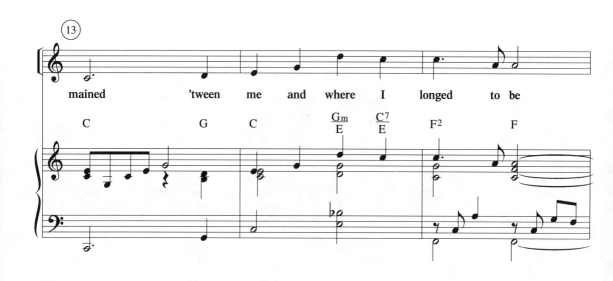

mained 'tween me and where I longed to be

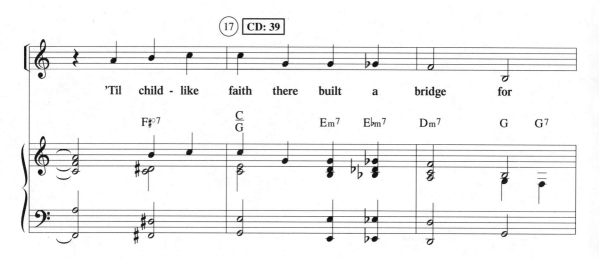

'Til child - like faith there built a bridge for

I glad-ly place my trust in things I can-not see. My faith still holds on to the Christ of Cal-va-ry.

CD: 40

end of where I'm bound I may not see,

I choose to place my trust in Cal va -

ry. My faith still holds on

Worthy of Praise

Worthy, You Are Worthy
Worthy Is the Lamb
He Is Worthy of Praise

Arr. by Doug Holck

**"Worthy, You Are Worthy" (Moen)
1st time: All, unison (opt. add congregation)
2nd time: S.A.T.B.

Arr. © 1990 by Pilot Point Music (ASCAP), Box 419527, Kansas City, MO 64141. All rights reserved.
This edition published in 1991.

78

In the Name of the Lord

PHIL McHUGH, GLORIA GAITHER and
SANDI PATTI HELVERING

SANDI PATTI HELVERING
Arr. by Doug Holck

strength in the name of the Lord._____ There is pow'r in the

name of the Lord._____ There is hope in the name of the Lord.

_____ Bless-ed is He__ who comes_____ in the name of the

CD: 51

Lord. His name will be wor-shipped for - ev - er:_____ Cre -

a - tor, Re - deem - er, and King,_____ the King_____

_____ of Kings. There is_____ strength in the name of the Lord.

molto rit.

Broad and accented

Broadly

There is pow'r in the name of the Lord.

There is hope in the name of the Lord.

Bless-ed is He___ who comes,_____ Bless-ed is He___ who comes,

He Takes Away the Sins of the World

KEN BIBLE and PHILIP P. BLISS

PHILIP P. BLISS and TOM FETTKE
Arr. by Tom Fettke

He bears our shame with-out re-ply-ing; He takes a-way the sins of the world. "Man of Sor-rows," what a name For the Son of God who came Ru-ined sin-ners

Both lamb and priest, God's Ho - ly__ One, He takes a- way the__

sins of the world. Lift - ed up was He to die;

"It is fin - ished," was His cry.__ Now in heav'n ex -

Alive—Medley

Arr. by Tom Fettke and Doug Holck

CD: 56 Broad and majestic

CD: 57

Slowly ♩ = ca. 69 — Dramatic

"Christ Is Alive! Let All Christians Sing" (Tom Fettke)

Christ is a - live! _____ Let _____ all Chris - tians

Lyrics: cause__ He rose, we__ too shall rise.__

Je - sus, Christ__ Je - sus is a - live.__

*"Jesus Christ Is Alive" (J. Hayford)

CD: 59 1st time

*"He Is Alive" (R. Courtney - B. Red)

Quickly ♩ = ca. 138

110

114

Remember

(Medley)

Arr. by Tom Fettke

With quiet reverence ♩ = ca. 66

* "Remembrance" (Tom Fettke, based on a hymn text by James Montgomery)

I re-mem-ber You and all Your pains And all Your love for me, O Lamb of God, my sac-ri-fice, who died up-on a tree.

** "We Remember You" (Kirk Dearman)

Solo or section

As we drink this cup, we wor-ship You; As we eat this bread, we hon-or You; And we of-fer You our lives as You have of-fered Yours for

Oo

Behold the Man

J. O.

JIMMY OWENS
Arr. by Joseph Linn

ris - en in glo - ry, com - ing to reign;____ By the Fa - ther ex -

alt - ed, crowned with__ glo - ry and hon - or.

Be - hold the Man,_____ King of Kings__ and

He Is Risen Like He Said

with "I Know That My Redeemer Liveth"
from Handel's <u>Messiah</u>

STEVE PETERSON
Arr. by Tom Fettke

He o-ver-came death's pris-on and He's ris-en from the dead. Dry all the tears of

sor - row, we have no grief to bor-row; Now we can face to - mor-row for He's

ris - en like He said. He has cap-tured ev-'ry fear and con-quered ev-'ry foe;

2nd time to Coda ⊕ ⑲

CD: 68

D.S. al Coda

See Him bruise the ser - pent's head with one tri - um - phant blow.

D.S. al Coda

CD: 69

CODA
Unison

(25)

Death, O death, where is thy sting, where is your dark do - main?

For you've been ren - dered

Unison

CODA

(25)

(27)
Div.

pow - er - less by His vic - to - rious reign.

He is not here, He's ris - en;

Div.

(27)

the gift of life is giv-en, For He o-ver-came death's pris-on and He's

ris-en from the dead. Dry all the tears of sor-row, we have no grief to

bor-row; Now we can face to-mor-row for He's ris-en like He said.

CD: 70

Ten Thousand Angels

R. O.   CD: 72

RAY OVERHOLT
Arr. by Tom Fettke

To Love and Die for Me
A Medley

TOM FETTKE

*"The Love That Died for Me" (Ferguson-Fettke)

My spir-it bows be-fore___ You In wor-ship___ and in love,___ And
all my soul a - dores___ You In maj-es-ty a - bove. Oh, ho-ly, ho-ly,___
ho - ly! How can this won-der___ be,___ So high and yet so
low - ly, To love and die for me!___ I___

138

*"To Think He Died for Me" (Newton-Fettke)

saw One hang - ing on a tree,____ In____

ag - o - ny____ and blood;____ He____

fixed His lan - guid eyes on me,____ As____

near____ His cross____ I stood.____ Oh, can it

be,____ up - on a tree The Sav - ior

Now and Forevermore

M. P.

MARTY PARKS

glo - ry pro - claims: "He is not here, He is ris - en!" And

(opt. solo)

heav - en a - bove ech - oes back the re - frain: "He is a - live ev - er -

CD: 78

He is a - live ev - er - more!

Div.

more!" _____

Je - sus is ris - en!

He is not here, _____ not here!